PUPPIES AND DOGS

Dr. David Sands

A SALAMANDER BOOK

© 1996 Salamander Books Ltd.,
129-137 York Way,
London N7 9LG,
United Kingdom.

ISBN 55349 00084

Distributed to the pet trade by Interpet Ltd., Interpet House, Vincent Lane, Dorking, Surrey RH4 3YX

1 3 5 7 9 8 6 4 2

CREDITS
Editor: Marion Elliot **Design by:** DW Design, London
Colour Separation by: Pixel Tech, Singapore
Filmset by: SX Composing Ltd., Essex
Printed in Slovenia

PICTURE CREDITS
Artists
Copyright of the artwork illustrations on the pages following the artist's name is property of Salamander Books Ltd.

Wayne Ford: 6, 16, 41, 55, 57

Photographs
The publishers wish to thank the following photographers and agencies who have supplied photographs for this book. The photographs are copyright of the photographer and have been credited by page number and position on the page: (B) bottom, (T) top, (C) centre etc.

Marc Henrie: 4, 5, 7, 8, 10, 11, 12, 15, 18, 19, 21, 22, 24, 28, 30, 31, 46, 48, 49
Cyril Laubscher: 20, 21, 22, 27, 28, 31(B), 34, 37, 40, 41, 42, 44, 45, 50, 51, 52, 53, 55
RSPCA Photolibrary: E.A. Janes, title; 42; Tim Sambrook, 14, 27, 39; Colin Seddon, 17; Steve Cobb, 20;
Andrew Linscott, 33,
61; Nigel Rolstone, 37, 50; RSPCA, 45; Ken McKay, 51, 56, 59
David Sands: 35
Interpet Ltd: Bernard Bleach, 41, 52, 53
Bruce Coleman Ltd: Fritz Prenzel, 47
Animal Photography: Sally Anne Thompson, 28-29
Jacket photograph ©RSPCA, supplied by RSPCA Photolibrary

Contents

Introduction

Dogs as pets

Dogs make great pets and there are plenty of breeds to choose from. They range from the tiny Chihuahua to the pony-sized St. Bernard. Each breed has its own special characteristics and it is very important that your family chooses the dog that best suits your lifestyle. Young dogs are rarely happy if they are left alone all day. If you are at school and your parents are at work your puppy could be lonely, unhappy and eventually become difficult to train.

Where dogs come from

Domesticated dogs, *Canis familiaris*, are descended from wild dogs and belong to a group which includes wolves, bush dogs, dholes, dingoes, jackals and foxes. They share common features such as long jaws and rows of well-developed teeth.

● *Above: In spite of its size, the St. Bernard is a loving, gentle dog that makes a loyal family pet.*

● **Above:** *The Chihuahua is the smallest dog in the world and its size makes it an ideal pet for the town or city.*

Dogs and early man

There is a great deal of archeological evidence from around the world to suggest that wild dogs were being domesticated by early man. It is thought that wild dog cubs were easily tamed when they entered human settlements looking for food.

Defending the home

There are cave paintings that show early man sitting around communal fires with dogs. These people probably used the part-domesticated dogs to help them to hunt and maybe also as guard dogs. Dogs were probably also used to help defend early settlements from animal and human enemies.

Domesticated dogs

Selective breeding
Several thousand years of selective breeding,
probably with a number of wild animals such as the
grey wolf and the jackal, has produced the wonderful
variety of dog breeds that is available today.

Different breeds
There are working dogs such as retrievers, pointers,
herders and hunters. In addition to these, a great
many ornamental and toy breeds such as the
Yorkshire Terrier and the Pug have been developed.

How modern dogs have developed
Modern dogs have been finely trained to guide the
blind, pull sledges, round up sheep, search for
smuggled goods, track down criminals and rescue
people from treacherous weather conditions.

Performing tasks
Most breeds have been developed with a particular
task or characteristic in mind. A gundog usually has
a waterproof coat, sharp eyes and a well-developed
sense of smell. Dogs that control cattle often have
short, powerfully muscular front and hind legs.
Hunting hounds are small with short legs, a deep
chest and a strong head. Racing dogs are sleek,

fine-boned and short-haired. Mountain dogs, used to rescue people in bad weather conditions, are usually massive animals with a large head and thick coat.

● **Above:** *Guide dogs act as the 'eyes' of their owners and help them to negotiate everyday obstacles.*

● **Left:** *Dogs have been trained to perform many tasks. Sheep dogs help farmers by rounding up sheep.*

Choosing the right breed

Gundogs

These include Golden Retrievers, Labrador Retrievers, Irish Red Setters, Pointers, Cocker Spaniels and Springer Spaniels. In general, these dogs are medium-sized and are cheerful and intelligent. They make good family pets, especially Retrievers, which are well known for their gentle nature.

● *Above:* This Welsh Springer Spaniel is a gundog. Gundogs are loyal and energetic and make good family pets. Spaniels are usually very healthy dogs and can live to a good age if they get lots of exercise and healthy food.

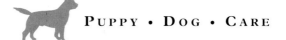

Hounds

These include Basset Hounds, Beagles, Bloodhounds, and Irish Wolfhounds. Hounds vary tremendously in size depending on the breed. Basset Hounds can grow to 35 cm (14 in) in height whereas Irish Wolfhounds are about 75 cm (30 in) tall! Hounds are lively and can make good family pets, although some of the larger breeds can need firm handling.

● **Below:** *The Basset Hound makes a very good family pet and loves children. Basset Hounds like lots of exercise and may wander off on their own, given the opportunity.*

Working dogs
These include Boxers, Border Collies, Welsh Corgis, Doberman Pinschers, German Shepherd Dogs, Old English Sheepdogs, Rottweilers and St. Bernards. Apart from the Corgi, which stands at 12 in (30 cm) tall, the dogs in this group are medium to large and need a lot of exercise and control.

Handling working dogs
The larger breeds in this group are very strong and can be difficult to handle if not fully trained in obedience skills. Working dogs are generally affectionate and protective towards family members but it is important to get your puppy from a good breeder to make sure it is just as good natured with strangers and other animals.

Terriers

This class of dog includes Airedales, Borders, Cairns, Jack Russells and West Highlands Whites. Terriers are small, strong-minded dogs and are happy and energetic by nature. They are also extremely alert and can make excellent watchdogs. Terriers tend to be easy to train and are extremely loyal dogs. They need daily exercise, but not as much as the larger working dogs and this makes them ideal pets for the town or city. With firm handling, terriers can make lovely family pets and are usually good with other dogs and children.

● **Above:** Boxers come from the group known as working dogs. They are quite large, powerful dogs and they need careful handling.

● **Right:** The West Highlands White is a terrier. It has a wiry, white coat that should be groomed every day. Its coat should be clipped occasionally to keep it neat.

11

Toy dogs

These include Cavalier King Charles Spaniels, Chihuahuas, Pekingese, Pugs and Yorkshire Terriers. As their name suggests, toy dogs are small but they have great characters. Toy dogs are lively and intelligent. They do not need a great deal of exercise but they usually demand a lot of attention from their owners.

Utility dogs

These include some easily recognised breeds, such as Dalmatians, Bulldogs, Shih-tzu and Poodles. Sizes can vary dramatically within each breed, especially in the Poodle group which includes small to fairly large dogs. Some, like the smaller Poodles and Dalmatians, can make good family pets while others, such as the Bulldog, are very strong and can be too difficult for children to handle properly.

● *Left: Two Cavalier King Charles Spaniels. These dogs are good natured and love children. They make ideal family pets. They should not be confused with the King Charles Spaniel which is very similar, but smaller.*

13

Choosing the right dog for you

If you are lucky enough to live in a house with a large garden or close to open fields, there are few breeds that would not suit your lifestyle. If you live in a busy town or city near main roads it is not a good idea to choose large or athletic breeds that need wide open spaces for exercise.

Handling

Most pedigree dogs make good family pets but some so-called 'intelligent dogs', such as Corgis, Shelties, Setters, Akitas and various hounds can be excitable and difficult to control once they have found a scent.

● *Left: All dogs, whatever their size, need regular exercise. If you live near a park, or open fields, you will be able to give most breeds of dog enough exercise to keep them happy.*

A small dog or a big dog?

Some of the smaller terriers and spaniels make excellent pets for families that live in a town or city. They are easy to train, need only modest amounts of food and can be handled by the smallest of children under parental supervision.

Large dogs

Large dogs need big homes, plenty of exercise and strong handlers. Outdoors, especially if distracted by scents or other dogs, large dogs could send young members of the family sprawling or pull a lead from a weak hand and run free.

● *Right: Mongrel dogs can make lovely pets. You might want to give a home to a stray mongrel dog from an animal shelter as there are many that need good, loving homes. Your pet's personality is much more important than its looks!*

Pedigree or mongrel?

Breeders of pedigree dogs usually have a clear idea of their animals' likely personalities. It may be difficult for you to guess a mongrel's final size or personality accurately. Discuss the kind of dog you want with your vet and get advice on the most suitable breeds.

Showing your pet

If you think you might want to show your pet professionally, it is best to buy a registered pedigree animal, which can be expensive. Of course, you can show any pet dog, including a mongrel, in a junior pet competition.

A dog or a bitch?

Male dogs roam more than female dogs (bitches). However, male dogs do not come into 'season', a time when bitches are 'on heat' and ready to breed. When bitches are 'in season' they should be isolated from male dogs to prevent unplanned matings.

Behaviour differences

Bitches are usually less aggressive and more homeloving than dogs. Dogs are more active when young but settle down as they get older. Male dogs scent and mark their territories with urine, but bitches are much less likely to behave in this way.

15

Understanding your dog

The dog's skeleton

The dog's skeleton is made up of two main types of bone; long bones that are located in the spine and flat bones which are found, for example, in the skull and pelvis. Although all dogs have the same basic skeleton, their bones do vary in size and shape from breed to breed.

● *Above:* *Dogs have a very highly developed sense of smell. They use scent to mark their territories and smelling is part of their greeting when they meet another dog.*

Sight

The dog's eye has upper and lower eyelids with a duct to drain away fluid and a third eyelid which helps to keep the surface of the eye clean. The dog's eye has developed from the time when packs hunted at dusk and light was limited. In semi-darkness the dog's eye reflects back light and this enhances any slight movements in the distance.

● **Above:** *Dogs have very good eyesight and can see well in semi-darkness. They have inherited this skill from their ancestors who relied on their sight for hunting at night.*

Sense of smell

A dog's sense of smell is much more developed than a human's. 'Sniffing' is a very important part of a dog's life. When dogs meet each other, smelling is part of their greeting. A dog also uses smell to mark out its territory. When your dog or puppy urinates it leaves its scent and, by doing so, marks its territory which other dogs can smell when they visit the same spot. A healthy dog has a wet nose. This helps it to detect smells.

17

Hearing

The ears of a dog vary in shape depending on the breed. Some are long and floppy, like the Cocker Spaniel's, while others are smaller and pricked, like a terrier's. Regardless of ear shape, a dog's hearing is much sharper than a human's. Your puppy or dog can detect high pitched sounds which you can't hear.

The dog's coat

A dog's coat acts as a protective layer. Some breeds have very fine hair while others have a wiry or coarse coat. There are also so-called 'hairless' breeds that have a thick, protective skin rather than a coat of hair. Some breeds moult while others, such as many terriers, do not. This is worth taking into account when choosing the ideal breed for your family.

● *Below:* *The Cairn Terrier comes from the Highlands of Scotland. It has an almost completely waterproof coat to protect it from the weather.*

● *Above: Dogs have very well-developed front teeth called 'canines'. These are inherited from their wild ancestors who used them for hunting. You should take your dog to the vet regularly to have its teeth checked and cleaned if necessary.*

Teeth

A dog has 42 teeth. They are specially developed to allow dogs to tear and chew meat and gnaw bones. Dogs have large fangs called canines at the front of their mouths. Wild dogs use these as a weapon to attack their prey.

Claws

A dog's claws grow continually and can cause your pet discomfort if they are not kept to a reasonable length. If your dog walks regularly on a pavement its claws may naturally wear down. Otherwise they will need regular paring and your vet will be able to advise you about this.

Making your dog comfortable

Taking your new puppy home

Ideally, your puppy should be about ten weeks old when it is taken from the litter. Any younger, and important social skills such as play and feeding, that it learns from its mother and the rest of the litter, will not be fully developed. This can lead to troublesome behaviour as your puppy develops into a mature dog. Take your new puppy home in a special carry case or wrapped in a blanket on your knee. Always have some tissues ready in case the puppy is travel sick.

House training your puppy

As soon as you arrive home, offer your puppy the chance to go to the toilet outside. If the weather is cold and wet, stand your puppy on some newspapers indoors. Praise your pet when it goes to the toilet on the newspapers. Ignore it if it soils any other surface unless it is outside the home. The puppy will soon realise that it must use the newspapers.

Going outside

Eventually, you can reduce the newspapers to one sheet at the back door and this can be removed altogether when the dog learns to go outside to go to the toilet. House training your pet could take up to four or five weeks depending on the breed of puppy and its age.

● **Above:** *Don't separate your new puppy from its mother and the rest of the litter before it is ten weeks old.*

● **Above:** *Spread sheets of newspaper on the floor and encourage your puppy to use them during house training.*

Settling your puppy in

Everything will be new and strange to your puppy, so try to protect it from too much fuss and confusion. Don't let younger brothers and sisters pester your pet as it will need peace and quiet to help it settle.

The first few days

Few puppies settle immediately on their first night and there could be some crying or howling. Your puppy will find life very different away from its mother and the litter. If you show your pet plenty of love it will soon happily accept its new family.

Your pet's bed

A cosy bed with a warm blanket will soon make a new puppy feel settled. You can buy various types of bed from your pet supplies shop. The most common types are made of moulded plastic or wicker. Plastic beds can be easily washed and cleaned and usually come in a wide range of sizes. Wicker baskets are less practical as young dogs often chew them.

Feeding dishes

Heavy pottery or stainless steel bowls are best for water and food. Dishes should be washed thoroughly every day, as bits of uneaten food can carry germs. Make sure your pet always has a bowl of fresh, clean water to drink.

A collar and lead

A leather dog collar can be worn indoors and in the garden. A check chain and collar will be needed for lead-training. Collars should be a good fit, and not too large or too tight for your pet. A name tag showing your telephone number on your dog's collar or a modern 'chip' are essential as they will help you to trace your pet if it goes missing.

● **Above:** *Before you bring your new puppy home you should prepare a cosy bed by covering a dog basket with an old blanket. All dogs need a space that is just their own and a basket will make your new pet feel secure during its first few days away from its mother and the litter.*

Feeding your dog

The young puppy

A growing puppy needs four moist meals a day. These can include scrambled eggs, boiled fish and prepared puppy foods. Most prepared puppy foods have been developed to meet the dietary needs of very young dogs. Read the feeding instructions on the tin carefully to check the amount of food that is needed by your breed. If you buy your puppy from a breeder you will be given a diet sheet for your new pet. Puppies of large breeds may benefit from calcium and vitamin supplements and your vet will be able to advise you about these.

CHECKLIST – *Feeding your pet*

- Wash your pet's dishes every day.

- Read the feeding instructions on your pet's food carefully.

- Ask your vet for advice on vitamin supplements for your puppy.

A balanced diet

There are many different types of prepared dog meals ranging from dried 'complete' foods to tinned foods. Older dogs need less exercise and may benefit from dried 'complete' foods, because they do not need as much protein. Younger dogs, especially healthy active puppies, require more protein in their meals and will benefit from a mixture of prepared foods and fresh food.

Feeding scraps

Dogs should never be offered food at your dining table. Any scraps (especially meat and vegetables) should be added to your dog's food dish. It is best if these are mixed with your dog's usual food, otherwise your pet could come to prefer your food and leave its own uneaten! Feeding your dog lots of tit-bits may make your pet overweight and unhealthy.

Treats

Don't give your pet too many treats. They make a good reward during training, but not all the time.

● *Left: A Golden Cocker Spaniel pup tucking into a hearty meal. Young puppies need four meals a day whilst they are growing.*

Questions *and* Answers

How often can I give treats to my dog?
Feed your dog small quantities of treats as part of their play and training sessions.

How much food does my puppy need?
Puppies need to be fed small meals, often. Talk to the breeder and follow the guidelines printed on your pet's food packets.

What sort of food should I feed my young puppy?
You should give your puppy four meals of protein-rich foods such as scrambled eggs, boiled fish and prepared puppy foods every day.

How often should I feed my adult dog?
Adult dogs can usually be fed either once or twice a day. You can give them a mixture of fresh and prepared foods to ensure that they get a balanced diet.

Will my dog overeat?
Adult dogs usually have tremendous appetites. To make sure your dog remains healthy, it is important not to overfeed it. Check your dog's weight regularly.

Can I give my dog scraps of left-over food from the table?
Dogs will eat most of the foods that humans eat but they should never be offered food at the dining table. Put it in their bowls instead.

● **Right:** *Treats will encourage your dog during training.*

Grooming and handling

Dogs should be brushed regularly to keep their coats healthy. Grooming will also help you to control your dog or puppy as brushing around your pet's head and shoulders is an important way of establishing your authority.

Brushing and combing

Some breeds moult at certain times of the year and should be brushed or combed every day. This is the best time to check your pet for skin infections and fleas. There is a range of grooming tools available. Some multi-purpose brushes and hand gloves or wire bristle brushes are suitable for fine or short-haired dogs. Most combs and deep brushes are recommended for long-haired or thick-coated dogs. Brush or comb through your dog's coat following the direction that its hair grows. Groom your pet's hind quarters and underside carefully, so that it learns to trust you.

● *Right:* *Grooming removes dead hairs and will help to make your pet's coat glossy, shiny and healthy.*

Keeping your dog clean

Most dogs need a bath sometimes, although puppies just need to be wiped over with a warm, damp cloth. Bathing needs to be done carefully. It is a good idea to ask someone in your family to help you to control

your dog. Some dogs enjoy a good bath and rub down while others behave as though their lives are at risk! If you make bathtime a fun family occasion it will help to put your pet at ease.

Bathing your pet

Run lukewarm water into the bath. It should be deep enough to reach the top of your dog's legs. Lift your dog into the water and wet it from its head to its tail. Once the dog is wet rub shampoo into its flanks and underside. A special dog shampoo is best, as most

soaps and shampoos are too harsh for a dog's skin
and can cause a skin rash. After soaping, rinse the
dog's coat thoroughly. If you use a shower
attachment the water should be slightly warm. While
your dog is still in the tub, drain the bathwater.

Drying your dog

Leave your dog in the empty bath tub for a few
minutes so that it can shake off some of the water
and then quickly dry it with old towels. Finish off
with a hairdryer set on low if you wish.

Clipping the coat

Some long-haired and terrier dogs need their coats
clipped regularly. This should be done by
professional dog groomers. Find a good groomer
through your vet or
from the telephone
directory.

Claws

If you walk your dog
on the pavement its
claws will probably be
worn down naturally.
If claws grow very
long they can make a
dog lame. They will
need trimming
occasionally with
special clippers which
you can buy from a
pet supplies shop.
Your vet will be able
to show you how to
trim your pet's claws.

● **Left:** *Dry your
puppy carefully.*

● **Above:** *Your vet will
show you how to trim claws.*

Questions *and* Answers

How often should I play with my puppy?
Play with your puppy several times a day for short periods of time. Puppies use much of their energy to grow and therefore it is better not to overtire them.

Is it safe to approach a dog I do not know?
You must never approach a dog without permission from the owner. All dogs, regardless of size, can bite.

Why should I groom my dog?
Grooming your dog keeps it healthy and stimulates its blood circulation. Grooming your pet will also help your dog to understand that you are in charge.

What kind of grooming accessories do I need for my dog?
Long-haired dogs benefit from combing and deep brushes; any brushes are good for short-haired dogs.

When should I bath my puppy?
Show puppies are bathed every week from about three months of age but pet dogs need only be bathed if they get dirty or muddy. It is important to use lukewarm water and a special dog shampoo.

How often should I groom my dog?
Daily grooming for a few minutes can be fun for both you and your puppy but a full brushing should be given every week.

Will my dog need to have its coat clipped?
Some dogs, such as terriers and those with long coats, need to be clipped to keep their appearance neat and tidy. You should take your dog to a professional dog groomer to be clipped.

Should I have my dog's claws trimmed?
Most dogs that are walked on the pavement will probably wear their claws down naturally. However, some may still need their claws trimmed occasionally, so ask your vet for advice.

● **Above:** *Your pet will enjoy regular play sessions. Young puppies can get tired very easily, so play with them for short periods several times a day rather than one long session.*

Training your dog

It is very satisfying to have a well-behaved dog. Training your pet requires patience and understanding, but when your dog learns a new command it can be very rewarding for both of you. It is important to have complete control of your dog when it is out in public places.

The basic commands

Try to teach your dog the basic commands. These are 'come', 'sit', 'move off', 'walk to heel', and 'stay'. Always make a fuss of your dog when it obeys your commands. Try to keep some dog treats in your pocket for these occasions.

Starting to train your puppy

After three or four months your puppy should understand most of the basic commands and will enjoy responding to them. Older dogs that are untrained may take much longer. Your puppy will learn best while it is enjoying itself. Training sessions should be short and enjoyable.

Rewarding good behaviour

Try not to become angry or disappointed with your puppy if it fails to respond to your commands as it will take many attempts to learn a new instruction successfully. Always reward your puppy with praise when it behaves well.

Teaching commands at home

Use a cheerful voice and address your puppy regularly by its name. When your pet has learned its name it can be taught to come when called. Stand a little way off from your puppy and tell it to 'come' using a confident tone of voice. You can also use visual signals such as patting your knee. To teach your puppy to sit, say 'sit' clearly, then gently and firmly push its bottom and back legs down into the sitting position.

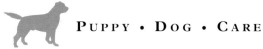
● **Below:** *It is very important to train your dog properly so that it is happy, well-behaved and under control at all times.*

Teaching commands outside the home

It is essential to keep your puppy or dog on a lead
when you are teaching it new commands outside
your home or garden. This will prevent it from
getting lost before it has fully learned to come back at
your command!

A collar and lead

All dogs and puppies should get used to wearing a
collar and lead. Most dog trainers recommend a
check chain and short, strong strap lead for walking
and training your pet.

Starting to walk on a lead

When your puppy is 12-15 weeks old you can begin
teaching it how to walk to heel on a lead. While
walking, keep your puppy close to your side. If your
pet pulls, tell it to 'heel' in a firm, clear voice and
then return your dog to your side.

Learning with games

Some of the most rewarding training can be gained
from 'throw and fetch' games. They are enjoyable
for your dog and can also be great fun for you. With
some effort and patience you can train your dog to
run and fetch a ball or toy bone and then sit and wait
for a reward. Some dogs respond better to these
games than others and you may be able to encourage
your pet to 'give' you the toy that it has brought
back. This game will encourage obedience.

Avoiding trouble

You should not allow a game of 'throw and fetch' to
turn into a tug-of-war. By training your dog you are
telling it that you are in control. If your dog grows
stronger than you and refuses to give up its toy, your
position of authority and your control over your dog
will be weakened.

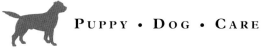

● **Above:** *Dogs and puppies should get used to wearing a collar and lead. Start lead-training your puppy early on.*

Questions *and* Answers

Should I smack my dog if it misbehaves?
The best way to train your dog is by giving it rewards for good behaviour. Never punish your dog as this will make it nervous and more difficult to train.

When should I begin to train my puppy?
You can begin teaching your puppy basic commands as soon as you bring it home. First you will have to toilet train your pet and then you can teach your puppy to come when you call its name.

Why should I train my puppy?
Puppies soon grow into adult dogs. To make your dog a happy member of the family you must have full control over it at all times, whether it is in your home or outside.

When should my puppy start to wear a collar and lead?
You should get your puppy used to wearing a collar and lead from an early age. You can start teaching your puppy to walk to heel on a lead when it is 12-15 weeks old.

What should I do if my dog has behaviour problems?
If your dog starts to behave badly, for example it becomes aggressive or barks all the time, it must be treated as soon as possible. Dogs that have behaviour problems usually get worse. Ask your vet to put you in touch with an animal behaviour expert who can help your pet.

● **Above:** *Always make a fuss of your dog when it obeys your commands and reward its good behaviour with treats.*

Providing exercise and toys

Regular exercise
It is essential that you give your dog regular exercise to keep it fit and healthy. It is important not to over-exercise puppies under one year old, because their bones and muscles are still developing.

Lead-walking
The best form of outdoors exercise is a walk on a lead, but you must have total control over your dog to keep your pet and others safe. When you are walking your dog or puppy keep it close to you and use the 'heel' command to keep it under control.

Playing with toys
Toys are a good way of providing exercise. Store them in a special box and always make a fuss when you get them out. Keep the toys for set times as this is a good way of training and controlling your dog.

Using toys
Toys that your pet can run and fetch are the best, as they teach obedience and encourage your dog to play with you for a reward. Every time your pet brings the toy back, praise it and offer it a treat. At first your puppy will ignore your commands. When this happens, it is best to put the toys away to teach your pet that it must obey you if it wants to play.

Choosing toys
Your pet's toys should be non-toxic and made of strong, solid rubber or special nylon to prevent them splitting. Puppies can soon swallow stray bits and this can lead to choking. Dogs also enjoy playing with soft toys and can find them very comforting. Rag-type toys are specially good for your pet as they will help to clean its teeth.

● **Above:** Solid toys should be non-toxic and made of rubber or nylon to prevent your pet swallowing stray pieces.

● **Above:** Some dogs find soft toys comforting. Rag-type toys can help to clean their teeth.

Breeding dogs and caring for the puppies

Breeding dogs

Unless you keep your dog specifically to breed from, you shouldn't let it become pregnant. Not only will you have the worry and cost of raising puppies but you will have to find each of them a caring home, which may be very difficult.

Pregnancy

A female dog (bitch) and a male dog (dog) are first able to mate at the age of 6 to 12 months old. The bitch is said to be 'on heat' at certain times and this means that she is ready to mate. The pregnancy will last for around 63 days. A vet can usually detect signs of pregnancy at around 22-30 days.

Preparing for the birth

A pregnant bitch requires extra food, vitamins and minerals. From the sixth week of pregnancy she should be fed more often than usual. About two weeks before the puppies are due to be born, you should make a warm comfortable bed for her to give birth in. A large cardboard box will do. The bed should be lined with lots of newspaper and placed in a quiet, private corner.

The birth

When the mother is ready to give birth, she will become restless and start to pant. This first stage of labour can last for several hours. The second stage is when the mother pushes out a puppy. A puppy is born about every 30 minutes. After each puppy is born it is followed by a placenta. This is what the puppy feeds from when it is in its mother's womb.

When to call the vet

Most bitches can give birth without human help, but tell your vet as soon as labour begins so that you can get help quickly if the mother needs it. The birthing stage should not normally last for more than six hours, although large litters may take longer. If the mother has been pushing for more than 30 minutes without producing a puppy, contact your vet.

● **Left:** *A mother guards her sleeping puppy. She will feed and care for her puppies for the first few weeks of their lives.*

BREEDING DOGS AND CARING FOR THE PUPPIES

The litter

There are usually between four and eight puppies in a litter. Shortly after the puppies have been born the mother licks them. This is to clean the puppies and keep them warm. The puppies soon begin to drink their mother's milk which gives them all the nutrition they need at this stage.

The first days of life

Puppies are born blind and deaf and rely on their mother to keep them warm, clean and well fed for the first 10-15 days of life. You should make sure that the mother and her puppies are kept warm, especially during this period.

Weaning the puppies

The mother will require a highly nutritious diet while she is feeding her puppies. She will also need extra vitamins and minerals. When they are very young, puppies tend to sleep a great deal. As they grow older they become increasingly active and need more food. Gradually the puppies can be weaned off their mother's milk onto solid food. This can begin from three to five weeks of age. When the puppies are eight weeks old they should be fully weaned.

● *Below: A new mother feeds her litter. Puppies rely totally on their mother for food for the first few weeks of life.*

Dog behaviour

● **Above:** *A group of dogs showing their pleasure at seeing their owner.*

Different moods

Dogs use body language and sounds to communicate. If you study your dog closely, you will see changes in the position of its head and ears, the 'look' in its eyes, the hairs on its coat and the position of its tail, according to its mood.

Showing feelings

When your dog's head and tail are up it is happy. It will wag its tail from side to side or even in a kind of circle when it is glad to see you. If its head is down and its tail is between its legs then it may be very unhappy. Sometimes this means your dog is being 'subdominant', which means that it is allowing another dog or a human to be in charge.

Guarding territory

When a stranger is in your home you will notice your dog's hair thicken and 'stand up', particularly on its back and neck. Your pet will often bark loudly and become very excited. This is your dog's way of communicating its desire to defend your house.

In the home

All dogs thrive on human company. They are pack animals, used to knowing their place within a group. Because of this, your dog may eventually come to believe it is 'human' or that your family represents its pack. However, you must always remember that your pet is a dog! Understanding this will help you to keep your dog or puppy happy at home.

● **Above:** *This Boxer dog is communicating its interest in something by pricking its ears forward.*

Mixing with other pets

Puppies will mix with almost any animal. Dogs that have lived in another home or with a breeder for a long time can be much more difficult to introduce to a new home where there is another animal. This depends very much on the breed and the age of the dog but a vet will advise on each case.

Introducing a new puppy

Introducing a new puppy to another dog has to be attempted with care. Few happy and healthy adult dogs will show aggression towards a puppy, but the introduction has to be taken slowly. An existing dog or cat will look on your home as its territory and will want to defend it. Any aggression from your existing pet should be discouraged and you should keep the animal under control at all times.

Introducing an older dog

When you introduce an older dog to a younger one they should be encouraged to play or exercise in an activity they can both enjoy. All food should be kept away from the meeting. All meals should be given separately for the first few days. Once there is full acceptance of the newcomer by the existing pet, meals can given in separate dishes at the same time.

● **Right:** *Supervise meetings between new and existing pets very carefully and discourage any aggression.*

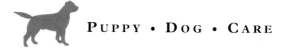

Dogs and cats

Older dogs, for example those that have been
encouraged to chase cats from gardens, will show
aggression towards all cats. Sometimes a dog may be
very friendly with your own cat and chase others
away from your garden but this is because it is
protecting its territory. Some dogs and cats will live
together in harmony with no problems.

Going on holiday

Taking your pet with you

Many guest houses and some hotels will take a pet dog as long as it it is under control at all times. You can find special books listing 'pet-friendly' establishments in your library or at your local book shop. Puppies rarely travel well and should not be moved unless it is absolutely necessary.

Using kennels

One alternative to taking your pet on holiday is to board it in kennels. Your vet will probably be able to recommend a good establishment to you. Inspect the kennels first to make sure that it is suitable and that the animals already there are happy and healthy. Make sure that kennel staff will exercise your dog every day during its stay. Remember that you will need to show an up-to-date vaccination certificate for your pet before it will be accepted. A good kennels will not take a dog without a certificate.

● **Above:** *Although you may feel apprehensive about boarding your dog, kennel staff are animal lovers and will do all they can to make your pet feel at home.*

Using a dog-sitter

Another solution is to use a 'dog-sitter', a friend, relative or neighbour who will keep a daily watch on your dog and give it food and exercise.

Making your pet feel at home

Kennel staff are animal lovers and they will always try to make your dog feel at home. You can help by bringing your pet's bed, blanket and toys with you. It is essential that your dog gets the same kind of food as you give it at home. This can be arranged with the kennel owners who will either stock the same food or ask you to bring some with you for your pet.

● **Above:** *A kennel maid exercising a dog. When you make enquiries about a suitable kennels, make sure that the staff will walk your dog every day.*

Keeping your dog healthy

First signs of illness

If your dog or puppy isn't interested in its food or loses weight, you should contact your vet. Any obvious signs of ill health, such as constant scratching, or running eyes or nose should also be investigated by a vet. Puppies with diarrhoea can become weak very quickly and should be seen by a vet as soon as possible. Adult dogs with the same problem need treatment and possibly a change of diet. Older dogs do not require high protein foods and special dietary foods, available at pet supplies shops or your veterinary clinic, can be better for them. Ask your vet for advice.

Ears

One of the most vulnerable areas in a dog is its outer ear. If infections are not spotted they can spread to the middle and inner ear and be difficult to treat.

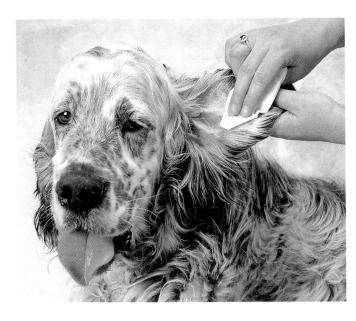

It is important to get your puppy or dog used to having its ears examined regularly for signs of

soreness or excessive dirt. If your dog has long, floppy ears it is likely to get more infections than breeds with small ears and regular cleaning is important to keep your pet healthy.

Eyes

Regularly clean around your dog's eyes with wipes. If your pet's eyes are watering or irritated or its tear ducts look blocked, contact your vet, as this can lead to serious eye infections.

● *Left and above:* *Regularly clean your dog's ears and eyes with wipes. Don't use cotton wool, as stray fibres can cause irritation and infection.*

Skin and coat

Your dog's coat can tell you a lot about its general health. When you groom your pet you will notice any changes such as bald patches, which could mean a skin infection. Your dog may be suffering from a mite infection such as mange or eczema. If your pet has a skin problem, you should take it to the vet. The sooner you identify a problem, the easier it will be for your vet to treat it.

Worming

All puppies and dogs must regularly be given medicine to protect them from internal parasites such as tapeworm. Puppies can be infected by worms before and after birth and should be regularly wormed up to the age of five months. After that they can be re-wormed every six months. Treatments for tapeworm can be given every year to an adult dog. Your vet will be able to advise you about suitable worming medicines.

Fleas

Dogs and puppies can easily pick up fleas. If your dog is affected, you can treat the problem with sprays and powders from your vet or pet supplies shop. You should ask for a preparation that will kill both flea eggs and larvae. Your dog should also wear a special collar to kill fleas.

Treating your pet's bedding

If there is a severe outbreak of fleas then it is essential to treat your pet's bed and any furniture that it likes to sit on with a spray or powder as well. This should also be a formula that kills both flea eggs and larvae. Another parasite, the tick, which is usually picked up in the countryside from farm animals such as sheep, can also be treated with a special spray.

CHECKLIST – *Pet health*

- Check your dog's ears and eyes every week for signs of infection.

- Ask your vet for advice on worming your puppy or dog.

- During grooming, check your dog's coat carefully for bald patches.

- Buy your dog a special collar to help keep it free of fleas.

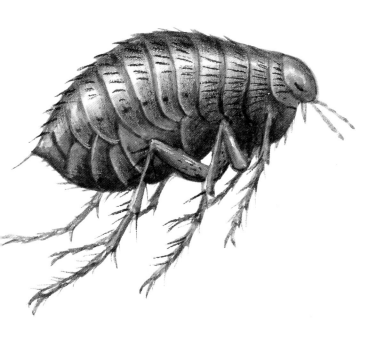

● **Above:** *A dog flea. This parasite can cause your pet a great deal of irritation and should be dealt with quickly.*

Questions *and* Answers

How should I look after my sick dog?
A sick dog needs special attention. It should be kept warm and comfortable. You will need to provide your dog with a quiet, clean place to rest and recover. Your vet will advise you about a suitable diet for your dog when it is not well.

Do puppies and dogs need vaccinations?
It is very important to make sure your pet is fully vaccinated. You should not let your puppy go out before it has been vaccinated. Mature dogs require booster jabs annually to top up their vaccinations.

Are there any diseases that could be transmitted from my dog to me?
Rabies, ringworm, roundworm and fleas can affect humans. You must take precautions to protect your dog from these diseases.

● **Left:** *Two vets examine a dog. It will help your vet to make the right diagnosis if you make a note of any changes you have noticed in your pet's behaviour.*

In an emergency

Moving the dog to safety

If your puppy or dog is involved in a traffic accident you should act quickly. If necessary, remove your pet from immediate danger by gently placing a sheet underneath it and lifting it to a safe place. Contact your vet immediately and find out whether you should visit the clinic or wait for the vet to come to the scene of the accident.

First aid

Check for the dog's pulse on the inside of its thigh. If the dog is having trouble breathing open its mouth and bring the tongue forward to check the airway is clear. If a wound is bleeding heavily, hold a clean cloth pad over it to stop the flow of blood. Keep the dog warm with blankets in case it goes into shock. A dog in shock or a lot of pain could bite without warning so you may have to muzzle your pet by tying a strip of cloth around its jaws.

● **Above:** *A cloth pad will help to stop wounds bleeding.*

Emergency first aid kit

This should contain tweezers, safe disinfectant, eye wash, antiseptic cream, adhesive dressing, antiseptic wipes and cotton wool.

Visiting the vet

Transporting your puppy or dog
Few pets enjoy a visit to the vet, although the scents and smells of the other animal patients will probably be a bonus to a young puppy! It is best to take your dog to the vet in a carrying case. If your pet is small or is still a puppy, you can take it to the vet in a special carrying box which will keep it safe and easy to handle while you wait your turn. Large dogs are more difficult to transport, although if you have a car a special cage can be fitted in the back. Your local pet supplies shop may have a selection of these.

Your pet's records
The veterinary clinic will keep a record of your pet's name, address and medical details. The record will list information about all the vaccinations and treatment your pet has had. The vet can use the record to check what medicines have been used in the past.

Meeting the vet
Always keep your dog or puppy close to you in the waiting room as there may be animals that are ill or difficult to control. When it is your turn to go into the examination room introduce your pet to the vet by name and explain what the problem is. You can also ask your vet to answer any queries you have about your pet's health.

Explaining what is wrong
You will probably know better than anyone else how your dog or puppy is feeling because of your close relationship. It will help the vet to diagnose what is wrong with your pet if you make a note of any changes you have noticed in its behaviour.

● **Right:** *Taking your pet to the vet for regular check-ups and vaccinations will help to keep it free of health problems.*

The examination

The vet will ask you to lift your pet onto the examination table where it is easier to feel the dog's muscles and bones, examine its mouth and teeth and take your pet's temperature. With regular examinations and vaccinations, plenty of exercise and a balanced diet, your pet should be free of health problems.

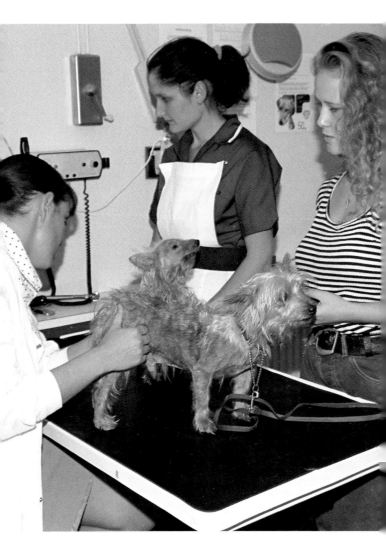

CARE CHECKLIST

DAILY CHECKLIST

- Wash all feeding utensils.
- Supply fresh clean water.

Feeding
- Puppies need feeding four times a day.
- Adult dogs need feeding twice a day.

- Exercise.
- Training.

WEEKLY CHECKLIST

- Grooming.
- Examine eyes and ears.

MONTHLY CHECKLIST

- Check claws.
- Bath adult dogs.
- Wipe puppies over with a damp cloth.
- Wash bedding and grooming equipment.

About my dog

MY DOG'S NAME IS

_____

MY DOG'S BIRTHDAY IS

_____

Stick a photo of your pet here

WHICH BREED? MY DOG IS A

_____

MY DOG'S FAVOURITE KINDS OF FOOD ARE

_____

MY DOG'S FAVOURITE GAME IS

_____

MY VET'S NAME IS

_____

MY VET'S TELEPHONE NUMBER IS

Index